# MORE

# MAGICAL SCIENCE

## MAGIC TRICKS for YOUNG SCIENTISTS

### UPDATED

By Eric Ladizinsky

Illustrated by Dianne O'Quinn Burke

LOWELL HOUSE JUVENILE

LOS ANGELES

*NTC/Contemporary Publishing Group*

Published by Lowell House
A division of NTC/Contemporary Publishing Group, Inc.
4255 West Touhy Avenue, Lincolnwood (Chicago), Illinois 60712 U.S.A.

Managing Director and Publisher: Jack Artenstein
Director of Publishing Services: Rena Copperman
Editorial Director: Brenda Pope-Ostrow
Director of Art Production: Bret Perry
Editorial Assistant: Jacky Jabourian
Typesetter and Cover Designer: Treesha Runnells-Vaux

Lowell House books can be purchased at special discounts
when ordered in bulk for premiums and special sales.
Contact Customer Service at the address above,
or call 1-800-323-4900.

Printed and bound in the United States of America

Library of Congress Catalog Card Number: 00-131153

ISBN: 0-7373-0513-4

DHD   10 9 8 7 6 5 4 3 2 1

# contents

# Is it "magic" or is it "science"?

When something cannot easily be explained, when it defies our understanding of the way things work, we tend to label it "magical." When you really think about it, don't most things amaze you? Think of the human body. Think of the way we are able to move and feel. Look at your hands. Notice the many ways you are able to use them—to gesture, hold things, pick things up, and feel things. Think of all the incredible things that have been created with human hands: the great pyramids in Egypt, automobiles, and even space shuttles! Human hands are truly magical instruments.

In ancient times, magicians were thought to possess many great powers. Today we know better. We realize that science is a way of explaining the illusions we experience in everyday life. For years, scientists have been the seekers of secrets—the secrets that make things appear to be magical. For this reason, they may be the greatest wizards of all!

This book will teach you some great tricks that seem to defy reason—until you read on to find out how and why they work. They are categorized by the particular aspect of the natural world they illuminate. For example, you'll learn to use the basic scientific principles behind gravity or chemistry to mesmerize your audience as you perform some truly astonishing magic tricks.

Remember that every good magician not only understands the trick he or she is performing, but also is able to keep the audience entertained and mesmerized. Follow the magician's code below to make your magic show unforgettable!

So, the answer to the question Is it "magic" or is it "science"? may just be: It's magical science.

## MAGICIAN'S CODE

**1** Magic, like science, takes practice to be good at. So practice each trick several times before showing it to an audience. All your movements must seem completely natural. Practice in front of a mirror until everything looks just right.

**2** Great magicians are also great storytellers. Capture your audience's imagination by telling them wonderful stories— by taking them on imaginary journeys to different times and places. For most of the tricks in this book, you'll find magical stories to tell. Use these, or if you prefer, invent your own!

**3** To help your audience imagine you as a magician, it helps to dress like one! For a magical effect, you can use a top hat, a wand, a long-sleeve coat, or a flowing robe with a scarf wrapped around your head like a turban.

**4** Make sure you have a show table to perform your tricks on.

**5** NEVER reveal the secrets behind your magic. Magic, once understood, is no longer magical!

# dinner at king arthur's

**Parental Supervision Required**

*If the blow be swift and true,*
*Then tiny atoms come unglued.*
*No longer held together fast,*
*They now can save—not break—the glass!*

 MAGIC

## You Will Need

- soft pinewood broomstick handle, 4' to 5' long (available at hardware stores)
- another stick (heavier and stronger than the broomstick and about 4' long)
- black and white paint
- paintbrush
- two sewing needles, each about 2" long
- small hammer
- two stem wineglasses
- red and blue food coloring
- two wooden or metal chairs
- water

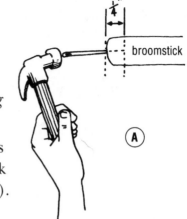

broomstick

(A)

## Getting Ready

*NOTE: Practice this trick outside before performing it in front of an audience!*

**1** Paint the broomstick to look like a wizard's staff (maybe black with white stars, or black with a white spiral—use your imagination!). Let the paint dry.

**2** Mix the red and blue food coloring with the water until it looks like red wine, then fill both glasses three-quarters full.

**3** Using the small hammer, gently tap the needles about ¼ inch into the ends of the broomstick, as shown (A).

**4** Set up the chairs, and adjust the distance between them so that when the wineglasses are on the edges of the chairs, the tip of each needle will lie on the edge of a wineglass rim (B).

**5** Once you have the correct distance, remove the broomstick—you'll need it to tell your story. . . .

## Performing the Trick

**1** Walk out in front of your audience with your eyes wide, your arms outstretched, and the broomstick in one hand. Say, **"I've been a sorcerer for a long time, and I've been known by many names. When knights in armor ruled the land, I was known as . . .Merlin."**

**2** Now walk over to the chairs and say, **"One night, during a grand dinner with King Arthur and his knights of the Round Table, Sir Lancelot, the greatest of all the knights, performed an amazing feat that surprised even me."**

**3** Then, holding the staff out, tell your audience, **"He asked to borrow my magical staff, and he balanced it upon two goblets of wine."** Place the broomstick needles on the wineglass rims as before.

**4** Pick up the larger stick, lift it over your head, and say, **"Then Lancelot brought his mighty sword down on the magical staff, shattering it into two pieces—*without* spilling a drop of wine. I have neither his sword nor his strength, but I do have . . . magic!"**

**5** Now bring the larger stick down as hard as possible on the middle of the broomstick (C). (For extra drama, yell **"Lancelot!"** as you break the stick!) The broomstick will break without moving the wineglasses.

**6** Look at your audience and say, humorously, **"It was a great trick indeed, but I was angry that Lancelot had ruined my magic staff, so I turned him into . . . a mushroom!"**

# SCIENCE

(D)

Hmmm . . . think about it. For the wineglasses not to spill, the ends of the broom-stick must have moved very little. How can the ends stay still when you split the broomstick in two? And did you know that the harder you strike, the *less* the ends move? To understand why, let's make a model of the broomstick, using people. Get five friends to stand side by side, holding hands, as shown (D). Your chain of friends is a lot like the broomstick, because the broomstick is actually a chain of **atoms** held together by electrical bonds.

Now, gently push on the center person in the chain from behind (tell your friends in the chain not to resist, but just to follow the push). You'll notice that everyone doesn't immediately move together. It takes time to get the whole chain going. Why? Because every object resists changing its position of rest or direction of motion (this **property** is called **inertia**). And because your friends are connected (by holding hands), the center friend is held back by the inertia of the others.

> **Inertia** is the tendency of an object to resist a change in the way it is moving (whether it's actually moving or not). In other words, things don't change their movement unless an outside force acts upon them.

This resistance puts a strain on the bonds in the chain (which your friends feel as a slight yank on their hands). As the hands of the chain's members pull on one another, each friend gradually speeds up, until finally the whole chain is moving together.

If the push you give from behind is too hard, however, the yank from the center person's hands is so strong that the other friends can't hold on. So their hands let go, breaking the chain. There is not enough time for either side of the chain to get moving very much, and therefore the people at the ends move very little, if at all. This is exactly what happens in the broomstick—the atomic bonds break in the middle of the stick, so that the very ends (the needles) aren't pulled on long enough or hard enough to move.

# halos

**Parental Supervision Required**

*Like ancient Greeks of times long past,*
*With their amber and straw dust,*
*Brisk rubbing transports charges fast*
*To electrify you, as charges must.*
*Force fields arise that float a crown—*
*Those Greeks would be startled, for it falls not down.*
*And though much time has passed since then,*
*And many marvels we have seen,*
*Our eyes grow wide with wonder when*
*We see such sights, as in a dream.*

MAGIC

## You Will Need

- piece of wool rug about 2' square (spare pieces are available at carpeting stores)
- sneakers with white or yellow soles (your size)
- pair of thick, 100% polyester socks
- thin plastic, coated with metal (such as Christmas tree tinsel, metalized wrapping paper, or space-blanket material)
- coat hanger
- scissors
- ruler

## Getting Ready

**1** Ask a parent or other adult to help you bend the coat hanger into a circle like the one shown here (A).

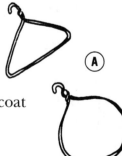

**11**

**2** Cut the metal-coated plastic into a strip about $\frac{1}{8}$ inch wide and two feet long. (If you have tinsel, it's already in thin strips, so just cut one of the strips to the right length.)

**3** Take the two ends of the strip and gently tie them together in a knot. Use the scissors to cut any tails sticking out of the knot. Now you have a thin loop of the metalized plastic.

**4** Put the thin loop, the coat hanger, the wool rug, the sneakers, and the socks on your show table.

## Performing the Trick

**1** Look at your audience and say, **"I once knew a great big magician named Ivan Ivanovitch. He had an amazing talent for levitation. His power to make things float was greater than that of any other magician. This power was *so* great that it became difficult for Ivan Ivanovitch to control it. His magic would seep into every object he touched, and wherever he went, things would begin to float. After a while things got worse, and even Ivan Ivanovitch himself began to float uncontrollably!**

**"So he ate, and ate, and then ate some more, until finally he got *really* big and heavy. Well, this helped him to stay on the ground for a little while, but eventually even his great size wasn't enough to overcome his magic . . . and Ivan Ivanovitch floated away."**

**2** Walk over to your show table and say, **"As soon as Ivan Ivanovitch was gone, magicians everywhere hurried to his house, taking everything in sight. They knew that anything Ivan Ivanovitch had touched still contained fragments of his great magic."**

**3** Now point to each of the objects on the table and say, **"By the time *I* got there, all that was left was the carpet on the floor, some old hangers in the closet, some tinsel from a Christmas tree, some shoes, and a pair of Ivan Ivanovitch's smelly old socks. I knew he had come into contact with all of these things and that they still contained the floating magic. Let's see."**

**4** Drop the wool rug on the floor, put the sneakers on, and slip one of the polyester socks over your hand. With the other hand, hold the tinsel loop.

(B)

**5** Bend down and rub the sock-covered hand back and forth across the wool rug for about 10 seconds, fairly hard. Then stand up, position the tinsel loop over your head as shown, and let go (B). The loop will magically float like a halo over your head! Then say,

> *Ivan Ivanovitch, feel free*
> *to gloat—*
> *Even your smelly sock causes*
> *things to float!*

**6** Have audience members put on the sneakers and the sock (on one hand), then have them perform step 5.

**7** If you like, hold the coat hanger and the loop in the free hand and rub the wool rug as before. Then position the loop over the coat hanger as shown in illustration C, and float the loop this way.

(C)

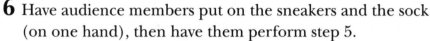

# SCIENCE

If you were to break an object into smaller and smaller pieces (smaller than you can imagine), you would eventually discover the **particles** that all matter is made of. These particles have names like **neutrons, electrons,** and **protons**. Many of them also have a quality called **charge**. Scientists say a particle is "charged" when it has certain definite behaviors.

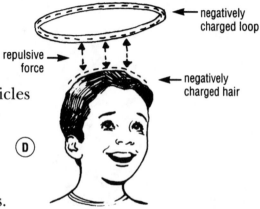

← negatively charged loop

repulsive → force

← negatively charged hair

(D)

There are two types of charges: One is positive (+), and the other is negative (-). Charge creates invisible force fields around a particle that affect other charged particles that are around them. Particles with the *same* charge (either +/+ or -/-) push away from each other. Particles with the *opposite* charge (+/-) attract each other. Most objects have roughly the same number of positive and negative charges. So, when two such objects are brought near each other, the objects neither attract nor repel each other. The positive and negative charges cancel each other out, so you don't notice any weird effects.

The ancient Greeks rubbed amber with wool and made small bits of straw move about without touching them. Since they didn't know anything about positive and negative charges, imagine how amazed they must have been!

In your trick, though, when you rubbed the sock on the wool, the rubbing stripped negative charges off of the wool and onto the sock. From there, the charges quickly spread out all over your body and onto the tinsel loop. Then, when you held the tinsel loop above your head, the like charges on your head and the tinsel repelled each other (D). This levitated the tinsel loop, allowing you to see the effect of the invisible force fields—a halo!

# pencil in a bottle ★

**Parental Supervision Required**

*There's a game of billiards we never see*
*Whose effects we feel constantly.*
*A game that's been going since the Earth evolved air—*
*The crashing of molecules everywhere.*
*If these crashings are used in just the right way,*
*The floating of water becomes child's play!*

 MAGIC

## You Will Need

- a clear glass juice bottle (similar to the one shown on the next page; you may need to experiment with different bottles to find the one that works best)
- sock
- pitcher of water
- pencil
- stiff cardboard
- scissors
- ruler
- blue food coloring

## Getting Ready

*NOTE: You should perform this trick after Halos, page 11, because it involves the same make-believe character.*

**1** Cut a square of cardboard five inches on each side.

**2** Add some blue food coloring to the pitcher of water to give it color.

**3** Put the pitcher of water, juice bottle, sock, cardboard square, and pencil on your show table.

## Performing the Trick

**1** Take the sock, hold it in front of you, and say, **"Do you remember this? It's the last remaining smelly sock of Ivan Ivanovitch—the giant guy who floated away. I'd like to see how much floating magic is left in this sock."**

**2** Pick up the juice bottle, begin rubbing it with the sock, and say, **"If there's enough magic left in this bottle, anything in the bottle should levitate inside it and not pour out."**

**3** Put the bottle back on the table and fill it all the way to the rim with water.

**4** Press the cardboard over the opening and carefully turn the bottle upside down, making sure no water spills out (A).

**5** Very carefully, slide the cardboard from under the opening. Amazingly, the water won't pour out.

**6** Now ask a volunteer to come up and gently push the pencil up into the bottle—right through the water's surface (B). The water *still* won't fall out!

# SCIENCE

The air around us is made up of huge numbers of **molecules** that are constantly colliding with each other and everything else, like little billiard balls. Look at picture C. The force of the earth's **gravity** pulls down on the water, which is why it normally pours out of a container held upside down. But there is another force pushing *up* on the

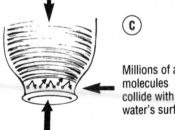

The water's weight pushes downward.

Millions of air molecules collide with the water's surface.

The air pressure pushes upward.

water's surface, and that force is air molecules colliding with the water's surface. The combined upward collisions of millions of air molecules produce an upward push. The upward push due to this **air pressure** is greater than the downward pull of gravity, so the water doesn't fall. So why doesn't this happen whenever you try to pour

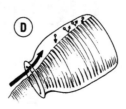

something from a bottle? The reason is that as you tilt the bottle, a space develops, allowing air to get behind the liquid that is balancing the air pressure from the bottle's opening (D). Now gravity has nothing to fight, so the liquid falls.

# clearly not here ★

**Parental Supervision Required**

*A glass disappears—its image just ends—*
*When strange oil spoils the way the light bends.*
*This bending allows us to see what is clear,*
*And without it we'd never know clear things were here!*

★

## You Will Need

- large Pyrex beaker (available at science supply shops, or check with a science teacher at school)
- two small, unmarked Pyrex beakers (the same size, and small enough to fit inside the large beaker)

- Wesson oil
- two towels
- small hammer

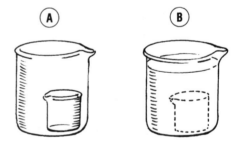

## Getting Ready

**1** Place one of the small beakers inside the large one, as shown (A). Make sure it's sitting near the side of the large beaker to make room for the broken pieces you'll put in later.

**2** Now hide the small beaker by filling the large one with oil. The small beaker will be completely invisible (B).

**3** Place the filled large beaker, the second small beaker, the towels, and the hammer on your show table.

## Performing the Trick

**1** Now it's time to tell your audience a tale of tears. Look at them sadly and say, **"I once heard a story about a remarkable woman of great compassion named Thelisia. It is said that once, while traveling through distant mountains, she came upon The City of Broken Things, a place where all the broken things in the world came—broken toys, broken children, and broken hearts. At seeing the ruined city, she sighed, 'So many people forget the broken things in the world.' So great was her sorrow that her golden tears formed a river that poured into a strange, golden lake. Legend says that Thelisia's tears were magical, and that any broken thing that was touched by them would become whole again."**

**2** Point to the filled beaker and say, **"I collected this mysterious golden liquid from what I believe to be the Lake of Thelisia's Tears. And now, it is time to test the legend."**

**3** Show the second small beaker to your audience, wrap it in one of the towels, and place it on the table.

Pour the broken glass pieces to the side of the small beaker.

**4** Use the hammer to *gently* smash the wrapped beaker, breaking it into small pieces.

**5** Now say, **"If these truly are Thelisia's tears, the broken pieces will disappear, and the glass will become whole again!"**

**6** Holding the towel, pour the broken pieces into the large beaker (C). *Make sure they do not fall into the small beaker already positioned inside the large one.* The pieces will disappear.

**7** Now reach into the large beaker and pull out the small, whole beaker, showing it to your audience (D). Pour the oil in it back into the large beaker, saying, **"Thelisia, the magic of your tears is still with us."**

**8** Wipe the oil from your hands with the remaining fresh towel.

# SCIENCE

Wow! Did you ever think that you'd be able to make something invisible? To understand how you did it, you first have to understand why objects are visible to begin with.

We see objects by the way they affect the light entering our eyes. An opaque (nontransparent) object reflects light that hits its surface. This reflected light reaches our eyes, and that's why we can see the object.

But light simply passes through transparent objects, such as glass. So how can we see them? When light passes from one material to another (for instance, from air to glass), the speed at which the light

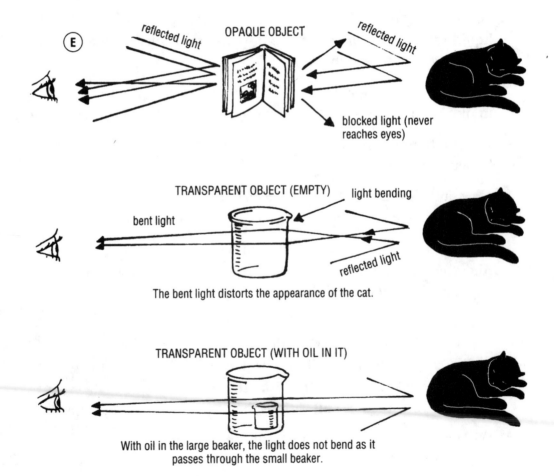

The bent light distorts the appearance of the cat.

With oil in the large beaker, the light does not bend as it passes through the small beaker.

has been traveling often changes. The changing speed causes the light to change direction, or bend.

Say you are looking at a sleeping cat (E). The light reflected off the cat travels directly to your eye. If you were to put the cat behind an opaque object (such as a book), the light reflected off the cat would be blocked. If you were to put the cat behind a glass beaker, the light reflected off the cat would travel through the glass. In doing so, the light bends, making the cat look a little distorted. This distortion tells us that something is in front of the cat—a glass beaker.

The glass beakers and the oil in your trick have something very special in common: Light travels at the same speed through both of them. That means that once the light enters the oil, it travels straight through the large beaker and the broken glass *without* bending. The light does not even slightly distort the image of the pieces of broken glass, so we can't tell they are there. The broken glass pieces are . . . invisible!

# ★ how to remove a gorg

**Parental Supervision Required**

*Round and round the coin will go!*
*If not too fast and not too slow,*
*A sudden sound—an eerie hum—*
*From deep inside the orb will come.*
*Tell your friends a monster's moan*
*Is what's behind the fearsome tone!*
*But what's the reason for the sound?*
*It's really science—how profound!*

MAGIC

## You Will Need

- large party balloon (try different sizes to see which makes the loudest sound when performing the trick)
- coin

## Getting Ready

**1** For best results, practice this trick first with a nickel, then with a dime, and finally with a quarter. In your performance, use the coin that produces the loudest sound.

**2** Stuff the coin into the balloon, then blow the balloon up until it's fairly tight and knot it.

## Performing the Trick

**1** Holding the balloon with the coin in it, walk out in front of your audience and say, **"Late last night, a mischievous, invisible, *tiny* monster named Gorg snatched one of my favorite magic coins and ran off with it. Fortunately, the magic coin has a way of trapping those who try to steal it."** Then, pointing to the balloon, say, **"The coin imprisoned Gorg by surrounding him with this balloon. If he would just let the magic coin go, he'd be free. But he's so stubborn—he wants my coin *really* bad."**

**2** Now grab the top and bottom of the balloon, as shown (A). **"Even when I spin him around inside, Gorg hangs on tight. Listen closely—you'll hear him howl!"**

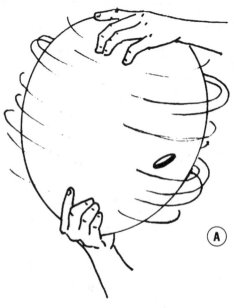

Ⓐ

**3** Start moving the balloon in little circles so that the coin runs around the inside wall of the balloon (A). As you gradually speed up this motion, recite this little poem:

> *I'll spin him at a dizzy pace,*
> *He'll get so mad, he'll scrunch his face.*
> *When mad enough, he'll start to growl*
> *And then let out his fearsome howl!*

**4** When the coin is circling as fast as you can make it, stop moving your hands. As the coin slows down, the balloon will suddenly give out a loud, wild sound. Then say, **"Oh little monster, don't you know? The coin will let you out if you let go!"**

**5** Challenge members of your audience to make Gorg howl (or to get him to let go of the magic coin!).

To understand what's going on, try observing something that's familiar to you—a stereo speaker. Put your hand in front of the speaker while music is playing. Do you feel a "buzzing" sensation in your hand? The cone in the speaker is vibrating back and forth, causing the air molecules close by to vibrate in the same way. These vibrations travel outward like ripples on a pond. Your hand feels the vibrations, but your ears *hear* them—as music. All of the sounds you hear are caused by vibrations of the air around you.

For the balloon to have produced a tone in your trick, the surface had to be vibrating, just like a speaker cone. The spinning coin caused the vibrations. But the vibrations occurred (and the "howl" was produced) only when the coin was circling at just the right speed. Too fast or too slow, and no sound was produced—why?

To understand, think about how a swing moves back and forth, and how even small pushes at just the right moments will cause the swing to move higher and higher. Pushes at the wrong moments will interfere with the swing's movement. So, you can think of the swing as having a natural way of vibrating (moving back and forth), reaching higher and higher.

The balloon, too, has a natural way of vibrating. As the coin circles around, it pushes against any given spot on the balloon's wall at regular intervals (an **interval** is the time it takes to circle around from one spot to the same spot again). If these regular pushes are just right (not too fast and not too slow), they'll match the balloon's natural vibration. As a result, the vibrations will get bigger and bigger (like the swing rising higher and higher), and you'll hear a tone—Gorg's howl!

# ★ "loosing" your marbles

*Under sparkling layers clear,*
*Precious gemstones disappear.*
*Though transparent the water seems,*
*Like black of night it robs their gleam.*

MAGIC

## You Will Need

- 1,000-milliliter Florence flask, with rubber stopper (you may be able to borrow one from your science teacher, or you can buy one from a science supply store)
- glass container large enough for most of the Florence flask to fit inside

- enough marbles (of all different colors) to fill the bottom of the Florence flask about halfway
- large pitcher of water

## Getting Ready

**1** Tilt the Florence flask so the long neck is horizontal, and gently roll one marble at a time into the flask (don't let the marbles roll too fast, or they might crack the glass) (A). Keep adding marbles until the rounded bottom of the flask is about half full.

Ⓐ

**2** Plug the top of the flask with the rubber stopper.

26

**3** Put the flask with marbles, the large glass container, and the pitcher of water on your show table.

## Performing the Trick

**1** Say to your audience, **"In an enchanted kingdom in a beautiful forest, there once lived two sisters named Megan and Caitlin, and more than anything else they loved to play and laugh."**

**2** Pick up the flask of marbles while showing it to your audience and say, **"One day their mother, Queen Julie, who loved them dearly, gave them an amazing gift. She gave them beautiful, colored crystal balls, which she said were enchanted. 'My dear daughters,' Queen Julie said, 'no matter how much time passes or how old you become, when you play with these magic crystal spheres you will become children again.' The sisters were delighted, and they invented all kinds of wondrous games to play together with the beautiful crystal balls.**

**"As the years went by and Megan and Caitlin grew up, they would often sneak away to the castle tower with the magic marbles so they could play again as children. The older they grew, the more precious the marbles became to them. Eventually, word of the magic marbles spread to other kingdoms. Great armies of men who had long forgotten how to play stormed Queen Julie's kingdom in search of the magic marbles. It was then that Queen Julie asked for my help."**

**3** Now place the large glass container on the floor and have your audience gather around it. Say, **"I told Queen Julie to first place the magic crystal balls at the bottom of a shallow wishing well in the middle of town, and then to invite the leaders of the armies to come and witness what would take place."**

**4** Put the flask inside the glass container.

**5** Pick up the pitcher of water and say, **"Then Queen Julie told the leaders of the armies, 'Before you lay siege to my kingdom, I beg you to watch what I do. I will show you how to find what you seek.' "**

**6** Ask the audience members to look straight down into the glass container. Then slowly pour the water into the container while saying, **"The queen poured water into the wishing well until the magic marbles disappeared."** As the flask becomes covered with water, the marbles will slowly disappear! When they've disappeared completely, stop pouring.

**7** Then say, **"The leaders gasped, thinking the marbles had disappeared. But the queen said, 'The magic marbles have gone nowhere—they merely lie beneath the surface. The same is true for all of you. Your magic also lies just beneath the surface. You need only to look inside yourselves to find the children within you.' The army leaders smiled and left Queen Julie's kingdom in peace."**

**8** Remove the stopper and slowly fill the Florence flask with water. The marbles will *reappear!*

# SCIENCE

Let's try and figure out why the marbles disappear. Look closely at everything that happens; there are many clues that will help you to piece together this amazing puzzle.

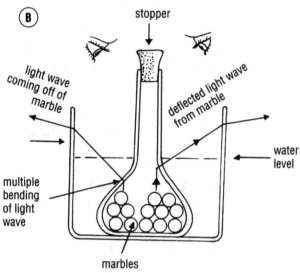

Ⓑ

stopper

light wave coming off of marble

deflected light wave from marble

water level

multiple bending of light wave

marbles

Think about it—the marbles disappear from view as the water covers the curved part of the flask, so the water must somehow keep the light reflected off the marbles from getting into your eyes (that's how you would see them). Obviously, the light isn't being blocked by the water—the water is clear, and light travels through it easily (and you'll notice that as you gradually change your point of view from looking straight down into the glass container to looking more from the side, the marbles will reappear). So what must be happening is that light from the marbles that starts out traveling straight up must get deflected by the water, change direction, and come out more toward the sides (B).

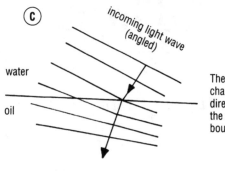

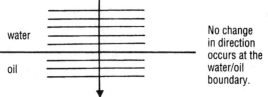

Why the light is deflected is the last part of this puzzle. In many ways, light behaves like waves in a liquid. The speed with which a wave travels through a liquid depends on the properties of the liquid. Waves travel faster in a lighter liquid, like water, than in a heavy liquid like oil. So imagine what would happen to a long wave traveling through water that suddenly crossed into a region of heavy oil (C). The parts of the wave that hit the oil first slow down and start to lag behind the parts of the wave traveling at different speeds. This causes the wave to change direction. If all parts of the wave hit the oil at the same time, all parts of the wave slow down together and it doesn't change direction.

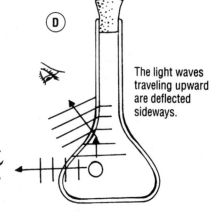

Light behaves the same way. Light travels more slowly in water than in air, so when light waves reflected from marbles cross from the water into the air they can change direction. Look at the shape of the flask (D): All parts of light waves traveling sideways off the marbles hit the water at the same time, so the light continues in the same direction. However, the parts of light waves traveling upward hit the water at different times, so those light waves change direction. Unless your eyes are in that direction, you won't see the marbles.

# 2d or not 2d

**Parental Supervision Required**

*When something's as thin as thin can be,*
*It starts to approach what's called 2D.*
*Objects 2D have only two sides—*
*There's length and width, but the height has no size.*
*Strange objects they'd be, when viewed just right—*
*For when turned on edge, they'd vanish from sight!*
*With no edges to stop them (no edges at all),*
*They could pass right through a solid wall.*
*But you'll find them not in this world's 3D—*
*It's in the mind's eye that 2D we see!*

MAGIC

## You Will Need

- sheet of white paper, about 11" x 17"
- sheet of thin black paper, 8½" x 11"
- table with a very smooth, flat surface
- glue stick
- clear cellophane tape
- sheet of white art board
- marker pen (any color you like)
- drinking glass, approximately 3" in diameter at the base (for drawing circles)
- scissors
- pencil

## Getting Ready

**1** Fold the black sheet of paper in half, then in half again. You'll end up with a square of paper four layers thick.

**2** Place the glass on the folded-paper stack. Then draw a circle around the base of the glass using the pencil.

**3** Carefully cut around this circle, through all four layers, to make four black paper circles.

**4** While holding the paper circles together as shown, carefully cut out one-quarter of the circles (A).

**5** Now tape the entire edge of the large white paper sheet to the table (make sure it's flat).

**6** Carefully glue the circular pieces to the white paper in the pattern shown (B). Make sure the edges are glued down well. It will look as though a white square is sitting on top of four black circles.

**7** Cut the white art board into key shapes and write some mathematical symbols on them, as shown below in C.

## Performing the Trick

**1** Now it's time to tell a story. Look at your audience and say, **"Some of the greatest magic ever performed has been achieved through the power of mathematics—amazing feats by wizards of the mind, such as Einstein and Newton. Mathematics can take you to worlds you can scarcely imagine."**

**2** Pick up the three keys and say, **"I have here three mathematical keys. Each key has an equation on it—a code that tells you how to enter another world."**

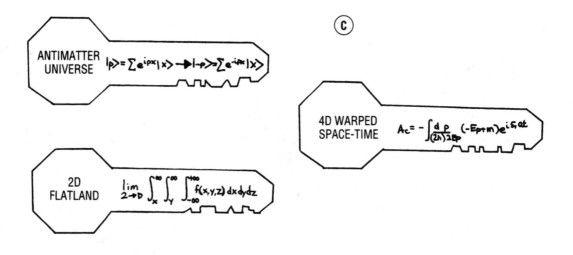

ANTIMATTER UNIVERSE $|p\rangle = \sum e^{ipx}|x\rangle \rightarrow |-p\rangle \sum e^{-ipx}|x\rangle$

Ⓒ

4D WARPED SPACE-TIME $A_c = -\int \frac{d^3p}{(2\hbar)^3 2E_p}(-E_p + m)e^{iS_{cl}}$

2D FLATLAND $\lim_{2 \to D} \int_x^{-\infty} \int_y^{\infty} \int_{-\infty}^{+\infty} f(x,y,z)\,dx\,dy\,dz$

**3** Show the key marked "2D Flatland" and say, **"I used this key recently to enter the world of 2D called Flatland. Everything in Flatland has only two dimensions. Objects there have a length and a width but no height. In other words, *everything* is flat! In our three-dimensional world, even the thinnest piece of paper has height—an edge. In 2D, *nothing* has an edge. If you try to see the edge of something that's two-dimensional, it disappears. Such objects can pass right through solid 3D objects, for there's no edge to stop them. When I left Flatland, I managed to get one of their two-dimensional objects into our three-dimensional world, and it's on this table!"**

**4** Invite audience members to stand around the table and look at the pattern you made, then say, **"This 2D square has only two sides—it has no edge."**

**5** Now have each audience member try to *gently* lift the square. They won't be able to, and they won't feel any edge!

**6** Have your audience sit down. Then pick up the other two keys and say, **"There are mathematical keys to many other amazing worlds. Study well and you, too, can travel to other worlds."**

# SCIENCE

Seeing isn't as simple as your brain just making a picture of what's there (a lot of what you see has to do with what your brain *expects* to see!). The patterns of light and dark entering your eyes have to be interpreted by your brain in order for an image (picture) to be created. Sometimes, different objects reflect very similar patterns of light, dark, and color. In response, your brain will interpret the pattern in terms of images it's most familiar with. For example, circles and squares are more familiar to your brain than circles with pie-shaped wedges removed. So, your brain constructs an image of a white square sitting on top of four black circles instead of four circles with pieces cut out.

# hole hearted

**Parental Supervision Required**

*If you know just where to stick a pin,*
*You can have yourself a great big grin;*
*For no one else but you will know*
*Why a balloon stays whole and doesn't blow!*

MAGIC

## You Will Need

- large colored balloon (that you can see through when inflated)
- metal filing tool
- long knitting needle (long enough to go all the way through the balloon from top to bottom)

## Getting Ready

**1** The tip of a knitting needle is usually curved or dull, but for this trick, you'll need it to be sharp. Ask a parent to sharpen the end of the needle by filing it down to a point. *The needle is dangerous once it's sharpened, so be very careful with it!*

**2** Blow up the balloon until it's tight (and transparent), then tie a knot in it.

## Performing the Trick

**1** Carrying the balloon in one arm and holding the knitting needle in the opposite hand, look upward and say, **"Long, long ago,**

there was a great king who forgot he had a heart. But it was not always so. He had spent most of his life defending his kingdom against dragons, evil wizards, and enemy invaders. To protect his kind heart during his many battles, he surrounded himself with an outer shell of fierceness. So strong was this fierce shield that even after his enemies had fled, the fierceness remained. His kind heart was trapped inside, unseen and unused."

**2** Make a sad face and say, **"He couldn't laugh. He couldn't care for his people. His kingdom was on the edge of ruin."** Then open your eyes wide and say, **"Until one day when a wise and gentle sorceress named Cassandra came to the king and said, 'Your Majesty, it is time to find your heart.' "**

**3** Show your audience the needle and say, **"Then Cassandra told the king, 'I have here a magic knitting needle that can pierce your armor of fierceness—and free your imprisoned heart—without harming you!' "**

**4** Now carefully push the sharp end of the needle all the way through the balloon, from the top to just near the bottom, as shown (A). As you do this, say, **"Cassandra pushed the needle into the king, and he was not destroyed. Instead, he turned to his queen and his people and smiled."**

(A)

# SCIENCE

You probably have never poked a balloon with something sharp before without popping it. And you know there's nothing special about the balloon or needle you used in your trick. So why didn't the balloon pop? Can it be there's something special about *where* you poked the needle?

In almost all balloons, the rubber is a little thicker at the top and bottom of the balloon than on the sides, where it is more stretched out. When you blow up a balloon, you force more and more air inside with each breath. The pressure of the air pushes on the balloon's walls, causing the balloon to expand (B). When the sharp tip of the needle pushes into the balloon, it creates a small tear. If the rubber near the tear is thin and weak (as it is on the sides), the air pressure inside the balloon will make the tear expand quickly—and the balloon pops (C)! But the thicker rubber sections on the top and bottom of the balloon can withstand the outward forces, so the tear *cannot* expand.

Once the sharp tip is in, the rest of the needle simply shoves the rubbery molecules of the balloon out of the way. In turn, these springy molecules push in on the sides of the needle, forming a seal (D). No air can escape, so the balloon remains blown up.

**(B)**

The air pressure pushes on the walls of the balloon until it is fully inflated.

What begins as a small tear in thin rubber quickly rips into a larger tear, popping the balloon.

**(C)**

The small tear in the thick rubber can't expand because the air pressure doesn't push hard enough on the rubber.

The balloon's molecules squeeze against the needle, forming a seal.

balloon's surface →

**(D)**

The air trapped inside the balloon can't get past the seal.

# gooplexity

*Like a waterfall frozen, it stills in midair—*
*A liquid called Gooplex transforms while you stare.*
*It changes from liquid to solid, and then*
*It changes from solid to liquid again.*
*And no one will guess how the change comes about*
*They may think they're dreaming—what they see, they'll doubt.*
*Such anguish you'll cause, 'cause humans can't rest at ease*
*With all these perplexing Gooplexities!*

## MAGIC

## You Will Need

- ¾ cup of cornstarch
- 2 cups of vegetable oil
- rectangular block of Styrofoam that will fit easily in your hand

- mixing spoon
- mixing bowl
- measuring cup
- any drinking glass

## Getting Ready

**1** To make the magic liquid, pour two cups of vegetable oil and ¾ cup of cornstarch into the bowl. Mix thoroughly until the liquid has the consistency of a light gravy.

**2** Now cool the mixture in the refrigerator. This will cause the liquid to become thick, like syrup.

37

**3** An hour or so before performing the trick, stir the liquid to mix the oil and cornstarch again (the oil will have separated over time). Make sure that the mixture pours easily in a steady stream. If it's too thick, let it warm up (by sitting at room temperature) until it thins out enough to pour easily.

**4** Just before your show, fill the drinking glass with the mixture. Put the glass, mixing bowl, and piece of Styrofoam on your show table.

## Performing the Trick

**1** Look at your audience and say, **"Have any of you ever been to the planet Morphous? It's one of my favorite worlds. Nowhere else have I seen such amazing shapes and forms. The cities are filled with incredible buildings—some round, and some shaped like seashells, Swiss cheese, or blobs of Jell-O—things we couldn't possibly build on earth! On the planet Morphous, there's no limit to the shapes that buildings can take. The Morphian people can make all these amazing structures because of a remarkable substance created by their scientists, called** *Gooplex.***"**

**2** Pick up the glass of oil/cornstarch and say, **"I brought some Gooplex back with me—it's thick and gooey like molasses, but it has very special properties. The Morphians, using invisible force fields, can cause a glob of Gooplex first to flow and mold itself into** *any* **shape they wish, then to become as solid as stone."**

**3** With your free hand, pick up the Styrofoam block and say, **"This is called Formita—it creates the invisible force fields that shape and harden the Gooplex. The Morphians said that I could activate these force fields by rubbing the Formita in my hair."**

**4** Now, with the glass in one hand and the block in the other, say, **"I don't know how to form shapes yet, but I think that I can change the way the Gooplex flows. Let's try it!"**

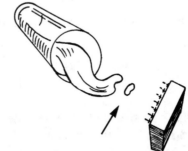

(B)

**5** Have your audience gather round, and hand the glass to one of them. Rub the Styrofoam block in your hair for a few seconds (this puts electrical charge on the block). Then have a volunteer *slowly* pour the Gooplex from the glass into the mixing bowl (B).

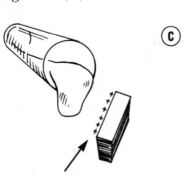

(C)

An excess of charges on the Styrofoam block will cause the Gooplex to stop flowing.

A piece of Gooplex may break off and fly toward the excess charges.

**6** As the Gooplex is being poured, slowly bring the charged Styrfoam block near the stream *but without touching the Gooplex*. The Gooplex will not only stop flowing, it will also appear to become solid. The liquid may even bend toward the block, and some may fly onto it (C)!

## SCIENCE

Let's try thinking like scientists to figure this one out. What do we know? First of all, the trick won't work with oil alone (try it), so the cornstarch must somehow control the way the oil flows. But how? The second thing we know is that rubbing objects together can sometimes produce an excess of charge on the objects (like when you rubbed the Styrofoam in your hair). So the charges on the Styrofoam must somehow affect the cornstarch particles, rearranging them in some way to stop the flow.

Here's the rest of the story. Each cornstarch particle is surrounded by a ball of oil (D). In order for the fluid to flow, these oil balls must be able to roll over and around each other like marbles (this is how a **fluid** moves) (E). When the charged Styrofoam is brought near the flowing oil, the positive charge on the Styrofoam causes the charges in each cornstarch particle to rearrange themselves. The negative charges move toward the Styrofoam, and the positive charges move away (this is called polarizing). The negative ends of the cornstarch particles bond (stick) to the positive ends of

The balls of oil roll easily over each other, forming a fluid.

**A fluid is a substance that can flow very easily. It doesn't have any particular shape. Instead, it takes on the shape of the container it's in.**

other particles, forming long chains, as shown (F). The oil balls around the cornstarch can no longer roll around each other without breaking the chain, and as long as the Styrofoam is near, the bonds are too strong. So, the fluid comes to a standstill. If you move the Styrofoam away, the bonds break, the balls roll, and the fluid flows again!

Styrofoam held at this end.

The polarized cornstarch particles cannot roll over each other because they're bonded (stuck) together.

# alien crush

**Parental Supervision Required**

*There's a beast I know who likes to munch
On hot boiling steam for breakfast and lunch.
He comes from a world all misty and hot
So you've made him at home in a boiling pot!
Take care when you feed him—he has a strong hand—
When he grabs the hot steam, he may crush the can.
But this beast is made up—it's the air that will squoosh
The can to a pulp as air molecules push.*

 MAGIC

## You Will Need

- 3 or 4 empty aluminum cans (such as soda cans)
- 2 Styrofoam coolers (one small and one large)
- large piece of dry ice (available at ice manufacturers or party supply stores)
- tongs
- adult assistant
- goggles (or other kind of eye protection)
- gas camping stove or disposable stove
- ice cubes
- eyedropper
- drinking glass
- food coloring (any color)
- water

## Getting Ready

*NOTE: Dry ice is cold enough to burn your skin! Always use tongs—never your hands—to touch it. Dry ice also evaporates quickly, so you'll have to get it just a few hours before your performance. Store it in the small Styrofoam cooler until you're ready to perform the trick (A).*

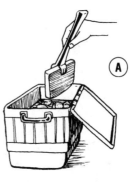
(A)

**1** Pour some ice cubes into the bottom of the large cooler until it's about one-third full. Then pour water into the cooler until it's about two-thirds full.

**2** Now make the water weird-looking by stirring some food coloring into it.

**3** Put the goggles, stove, aluminum cans, eyedropper, and glass of water on your show table.

**4** Just before you're ready to do the trick, and without letting anyone see you, take the large piece of dry ice from the small cooler (using the tongs), and put it into the large cooler. The water will bubble, and a mist will form (B). Quickly close the lid.

## Performing the Trick

**1** Bring out the large cooler and tongs, set them on your show table, and say, **"As a magician who travels to other worlds quite often, I rely on my alien friends to give me a place to stay while I visit. So, when they visit earth, I'm sort of obligated to return the favor. Right now, I have a little beast called Kuwata-D staying with me. He comes from Balino-va, a planet of hot liquid and gas—kind of like the planet Jupiter in our own solar system. Actually, Kuwata-D is staying in the cooler you see before you."**

**2** Walk over to the large cooler, grab the lid, and say, **"To make Kuwata-D feel at home during his stay, I've tried to re-create the conditions on his planet in this container."**

**3** Lift the lid, and mist will pour out over the sides. Say, **"He should be really hungry by now—it's about lunchtime on Balinova."**

**4** Ask a parent or other adult to assist you in making Kuwata-D's "lunch." While you put two to three eyedroppers full of water in one can, have your assistant turn the stove on low heat and place the can (using the tongs) over the flame (C).

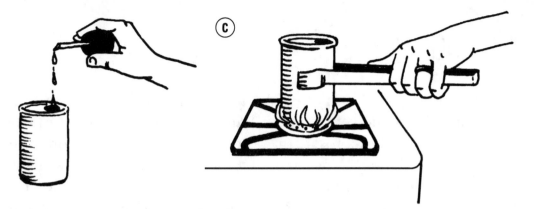

**5** As the can with water is heating up, look at the audience and say, **"The little beastie Kuwata-D eats pure hot steam. He uses the energy in steam the way we use energy in food. You have to be very careful when you feed him, because this beast is very strong. He has to be strong to withstand Balinova's powerful gravity, which would crush most of us. So when you give him some steam to eat, make sure he doesn't get hold of you, or he may crush your hand along with the can!"**

**6** Put on the goggles.

**7** When a whiff of steam appears above the hot can, pick up the can with the tongs, turn it upside down, and shake out any remaining water. Then, while thrusting the opening of the can into the cold water in the large cooler, say, **"Hey, Kuwata-D. It's lunchtime!"** There will be a loud "whump" as the can is crushed. Pull it out, show it to your audience, and say, **"Hmmm—I guess he was really hungry!"** (D)

**8** Have your cooking assistant make other cans of steam, and let volunteers from the audience feed Kuwata-D the same way, using the tongs and goggles. (If the liquid in the cooler stops bubbling, add some more dry ice.)

# SCIENCE

There was no obvious powerful force pushing on the can, so what crushed it? Would you believe it's the air? Remember Pencil in a Bottle (page 15)? The air is made of little molecules that are constantly colliding with everything. An empty can normally has just as many air molecules pounding on it from the outside as from the inside. In other words, there is just as much force pushing on the *outside* of the can as there is pushing on the *inside* of the can, so the can's walls stay put. However, if enough of the air from the inside were somehow removed, there would be less force pushing out than pushing in. As a result, the can would collapse inward. This is just what happened in your trick.

But how did you remove the air from inside the can? When you heated the water, it turned from a liquid into a gas (**steam**). A lot of the air in the can collided with these water molecules and got knocked out of the can (through the opening). The can didn't collapse immediately because the water molecules inside were themselves slamming into the walls and pushing them outward. But as soon as you cooled the can by dunking it into cold water, the steam condensed back into liquid drops. As a result, the water molecules were no longer pounding against the inside of the can. And with much of the air inside already knocked out, there was neither steam nor air to push out the sides of the walls. The outside air pressure could then crush the can inward.

> Like the air, **steam** is a kind of gas. It is made of heated water molecules that fly around freely.

44

# seesaw a ghost

*Two shy little ghosts come out to play.*
*We know that they're there by the candlestick's sway.*
*They laugh and they giggle and make quite a fuss*
*As they rock on a seesaw while hiding from us.*

MAGIC

**Mechanics**

## You Will Need

- two tall drinking glasses
- a cylindrical candle, about 10" tall (do not use a tapered candle)
- a thin metal rod, about 1/16" in diameter and 4" long
- knife
- matches
- two saucers
- pliers
- ruler

## Getting Ready

**1** Have a parent or other adult use the knife to cut away the bottom of the candle so that it looks like the top—that is, with the candlewick sticking out (A).

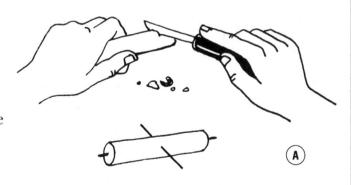

(A)

**2** Next, using the ruler, find the center of the candle as accurately as you can. Make a small mark there with your fingernail.

**3** Now hold one end of the metal rod with the pliers and push it right through the center of the candle (A).

**4** Rest the metal rod on the rims of the two glasses, as shown (B). Is the candle balanced? If one end dips lower than the other, trim a little wax off that end until the candle balances horizontally. When balanced (that is, when the metal rod is in the exact center of the candle), the candle should rock back and forth very easily, like a seesaw.

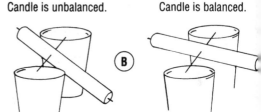

Candle is unbalanced.　　　Candle is balanced.

**5** Set up your candle seesaw on your show table. Put one saucer under each end of the candle (to catch dripping wax), and have your matches ready.

## Performing the Trick

**1** Walk to the table, look at your audience, and say, **"I know two very shy little ghosts named Bloop and Gloop. Bloop and Gloop love to play, but they're so shy they won't come out to play if they think anyone can see them. But there's one time when they're certain no one can see them.**

   **"You see, Bloop and Gloop look like little glowing flames. So when there's candlelight, Bloop and Gloop can come out to play because they can hide themselves inside the glow of the candle's flame. Have you ever seen a candle flame wiggle? It was probably Bloop or Gloop laughing from inside the flame."**

**2** Show the candle seesaw to your audience and say, **"Well, I've created a toy for Bloop and Gloop that I know they won't be able to resist. It's a seesaw—a candle seesaw. Let's turn out the lights and see if we can get Bloop and Gloop to come out and play."**

**3** While you or an adult light both ends of the candle, lightly tap on one end of the seesaw to get it started, without letting anyone see you do so. Have someone turn out the lights.

**4** Once the candle ends start to drip, say, **"Come on out, Bloop and Gloop! Look, it's a seesaw!"** Slowly back away from the table and stare intensely at the seesaw. Then quietly whisper to your audience, **"Look, there they are! If you watch very carefully, you might be able to see their little ghost feet pushing off."** The seesaw will mysteriously rock up and down as long as the candle ends stay lit (C).

**5** After a few moments, look at your audience and say, **"Let's sneak up on them really carefully and then blow out the candles. We should be able to see the little glowing ghosts for a moment before they run away."**

**6** Get a group of volunteers to sneak up on Bloop and Gloop with you. When you're close to the seesaw, whisper, **"Ready? Blow!"** and blow out the candles. Quickly turn your head as if you're watching them run away and say, **"Did you see them? I bet they're laughing now."**

# SCIENCE

Think about the last time you were on a seesaw. How did you keep it going? Well, every time you came close to the ground, you pushed upward with your feet. This pushed your side of the seesaw up, and then your partner pushed his or her side up, and so on. But where do the "pushes" come from to keep the *candle* seesaw moving? Maybe it's the pushing of little ghost feet!

To understand what's going on, look carefully at the way the wax droplets fall from the ends of the candle. As a droplet stretches and then breaks away, it provides a little upward snap, like a breaking rubber band. That snap is actually a small force that pushes on that end of the candle. Look at the timing of the drops breaking off, and you'll see how the alternating upward forces keep the seesaw going. When you blow out the candles, the seesaw motion stops.

# magic touch

**Parental Supervision Required**

*At times your senses will fail,*
*And illusion and doubt will prevail.*
*A story you will tell*
*Of casting a spell,*
*And they'll see what they can't explain.*
*Their fingers move close*
*As they get a dose*
*Of feelings that mislead their brain.*

MAGIC

## You Will Need

- fruit juice (any kind)
- food coloring (any color)
- wineglass (or any oddly shaped glass)
- long table (like a dining table)
- black tablecloth
- ruler
- volunteer
- enough chairs to seat your audience members around the table
- some interesting things to put on the table (a candle, matches, some old books, a magic wand—anything that creates a magical feeling)

## Getting Ready

*NOTE: If a long table isn't available or there are too many people in your audience to be seated, just spread a black tablecloth out on the floor and have people sit in a circle on it. You'll then have to be extra careful not to spill the fruit-juice glass, and **do not** use a candle!*

**1** Cover the table with the black tablecloth, then carefully place the objects you've chosen on the table. Next, put the chairs around the table, making sure that there is a chair at each end of the table.

**2** Fill the wineglass with juice, and mix in some food coloring to make it look like a weird magic potion.

**3** Place the glass at one end of the table and the ruler at the other end. For mood, light the candle and, if it's late afternoon or evening, dim any electric lights.

## Performing the Trick

**1** Start by asking a volunteer to sit at the end of the table where the ruler is.

**2** Now, you sit at the end of the table where the fruit-juice glass is, and have the rest of your audience fill the empty seats (A).

**3** Lift the glass in one hand and look around the table, saying, **"I'm sure you've all heard of magic potions that create great strength or wisdom. Well, the potion I've made makes anyone who drinks it obey my every thought."**

**4** Next, carefully hand the magic potion to the person next to you, asking him or her to pass the glass to the next person, then the next, until it reaches your volunteer near the ruler.

**5** Then, with your eyes open wide, look across the table at the volunteer and say,
> *Now drink my strange brew*
> *And my bidding you'll do!*

**6** After the volunteer drinks the potion, ask him to clasp his hands together, interlocking his fingers and thumbs. Then, have the volunteer extend his index fingers as shown, without unclasping his hands (B). (The volunteer's forearms and hands should be sitting on the table, with the insides of his wrists touching his ribs.)

**7** Now ask the person next to the volunteer to use the ruler to make sure the volunteer's fingertips are one inch apart.

**8** Opening your eyes wide again, stare at your volunteer and say, **"Keep your eyes locked on mine, and without looking at your hands, try to keep your fingertips from moving. With my thoughts, I will make your fingers obey my command—I will make them touch."**

**9** After a little while, your volunteer's fingers will move closer and closer together until they eventually touch. Say, **"My thoughts are powerful, indeed—look at your fingertips!"** Your volunteer will be surprised to see his fingertips touching, because he will not have felt them getting closer.

## SCIENCE

Do you think it really was the power of your thoughts that made your volunteer touch his fingertips together? If so, then you've just experienced something you've never seen before—a kind of "mind force." But before a scientist can accept that a weird, unfamiliar idea like "mind force" explains something he or she has experienced, the scientist will try to understand that experience in terms of ideas that are already familiar and accepted. So, let's try a little experiment to see if we can piece together an explanation.

Clasp your hands together. Now extend your index fingers and separate them just the way your volunteer did. Close your eyes and try to keep your fingers absolutely still. After a while, you'll feel them touch. This is exactly what happened to your volunteer, yet no one was trying to control *you* with thoughts.

Now try it again, this time keeping your eyes on your fingertips. You'll soon discover the real secret: If you try to keep your fingers one inch apart, it becomes harder and harder to do so. Why? Because clasping your hands in this way puts a lot of strain on the muscles in your fingers. These muscles become more tired as time passes. The only way to reduce the strain on your finger muscles is to allow your fingers to move closer together. The funny thing is that when your finger muscles are tired, your fingers feel the same way when they're close as they do when they're farther apart. When you can't see your fingers moving together (because your eyes are closed or you aren't looking), your brain thinks that since your fingers *feel* the same, they're the same distance apart as they were before. And that's how you—and your volunteer—are fooled!

# ★ a matched set

**Parental Supervision Required**

*They rise and fall—always together—*
*As the old one had foretold.*
*The spark of their lives held forever*
*By bonds that could not grow cold.*
*Three matches were made—their dance told the tale*
*Of the sons whose lives gave them light.*
*Every night they were watched and their glow never failed,*
*And the father's eyes were made bright.*

MAGIC

## You Will Need

- 3 paper matches (the kind in a matchbook)
- fluorescent paint (any color will do)
- small paintbrush
- desk (or table) lamp
- black light bulb that fits the lamp
- volunteer
- clear glass bottle (one that fits your finger snugly, as shown on page 55)
- extension cord
- water
- table
- chair
- music (optional; dreamy electronic music would work well with this trick!)

## Getting Ready

*NOTE: It's important to perform this trick in a room that can be made very dark.*

**1** Lightly paint the heads of the matches with the fluorescent paint (use just enough paint to cover the match heads). Let dry.

**2** *Unplug the desk lamp*, then remove the light bulb and replace it with the black light bulb.

**3** Place the bottle, the three matches, and the desk lamp on your show table.

**4** Fill the bottle to the top with water.

**5** Plug the desk lamp into a nearby outlet and turn it on. Just before performing the trick, turn off all other lights in the room.

## Performing the Trick

**1** Standing before your audience, say, **"There once was a maker of magic matches who lived in a quiet forest village. His matches lit the lamps and sparked the fires that lighted the homes and warmed the people of his village. This match-maker had three sons, named Ivan Ivanovitch, Eric, and Nicolas."** (Remember that you don't have to use the names given here! You can use the names of your brothers or sisters or friends, instead. It's fun for your audience to hear their names in your story!)

**2** Pick up the three painted matches, hold them in front of you (A), and say, **"The match-maker made three magic matches—one for each of his sons. The moment each son was born, the match made for him sparked into a flame, and from that day on the match became magically linked with the child. Growing up, the three brothers were very close to each other.**

**"The day came when they had to say good-bye to their parents. Now grown up, the brothers decided to go on a great journey to an unknown land. The match-maker worried about them, but he knew**

that by watching how the three magic matches moved in a bottle of water, he could tell if his sons were all right."

**3** Sit at the table and drop each painted match into the bottle, with the match head down. Say, **"Imagine the match-maker sitting late at night watching the matches dance."**

**4** Now push your finger into the bottle (it should be a snug fit). The glowing matches will sink. If you pull your finger up (but not out) of the bottle, the matches will rise again. Do this pushing and pulling several times, saying, **"Look! Ivan, Eric, and Nicolas** [or whatever names you choose] **are journeying safely together still!"**

# SCIENCE

To understand why you can make the matches float or sink when you want them to, you first have to understand why some objects float while others sink. For an object to sink, an amount of water equal to the size of the object has to move *out of the way* to make room for it. Where does the water go to make room? It can't move down, because there's already water there. It can't move sideways, either, because the walls of the container are in the way. The only direction left for the water to move is up. But remember that gravity is pulling everything down, so how can the water move *up* all by itself? To answer that question, think about a seesaw. When two kids sit on one end of the seesaw

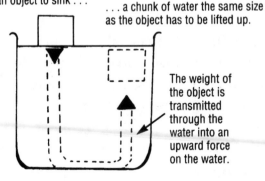

For an object to sink . . .

. . . a chunk of water the same size as the object has to be lifted up.

The weight of the object is transmitted through the water into an upward force on the water.

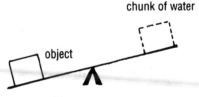

Ⓑ

chunk of water

object

The object will sink if it is heavier than a chunk of water the same size.

(without pushing up or down on it), gravity pulls the heavier end down, and that in turn pushes the lighter end up. The same thing happens when an object sinks in water: The downward movement of the object results in an upward push on the water (B). The amount of water pushed is equal to the size of the object. If that chunk of water is *lighter* than the object, the object pushes the water up easily and sinks. If that chunk of water is *heavier* than the object, the object can't push the water out of the way, so it floats.

In your trick, the matches floated at first, so each must be lighter than a chunk of water the same size. Then why did the matches sink when you pushed your finger into the bottleneck? That action must somehow have made them heavier. Here's how: When you pushed your finger in, you also squeezed a pocket of air above the water (C). That air pocket in turn squeezed the water below it, which (believe it or not!) forced water into the paper fibers in the matches. With water now soaked into their fibers, the matches were heavier and so were able to sink. Pulling *up* on your finger created a suction that pulled the water back out of the match fibers, making them light enough to float again!

# ★ no powder puff

**Parental Supervision Required**

*Powdered*
*Stuff*
*A puff*
*A plume*
*BOOM!*

MAGIC

## You Will Need

- coffee can with plastic lid
- hammer and nail (or something else to make a small hole in the can)
- plastic tube, 1" long and ¼" wide
- rubber tube, 18" long and slightly more than ¼" wide (so it fits snugly over the plastic tube)
- candle that fits inside the coffee can
- matches
- rubber cement
- colored glass stones or rhinestones (or anything that looks like jewels)
- paper
- pen
- cellophane tape
- scissors
- small glass bottle
- very fine sifted flour
- spoon
- two pairs of goggles (or other kind of eye protection)
- volunteer

## Getting Ready

*NOTE: To get the best results, experiment with different amounts of flour before performing this trick. Also, be sure you and your volunteer wear goggles when indicated, and perform the trick 10 feet or more away from your audience.*

**1** Have a parent or other adult make a hole near the bottom of the can, as shown (A). The hole should be large enough so that the plastic tube will fit snugly.

**2** Using the rubber cement, glue the plastic tube in place in the hole. Put extra cement around the hole to seal it.

**3** Now put some rubber cement on the outside end of the plastic tube and slide the rubber tube about ¼ inch over it, as shown (A).

**4** With an adult's help, light the match, then carefully heat the base of the candle. When it starts to melt, quickly stick the candle to the bottom of the can. Hold it there until the wax hardens again.

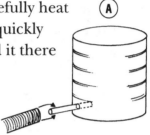

**5** Place the colored glass stones in the bottom of the can, on the side opposite the tube.

**6** Pour some flour into the small glass bottle. With the paper, pen, and scissors, make a label that says "FREEZE-DRIED TORNADO POWDER." Use the tape to stick the label to the bottle.

**7** Put the coffee can, lid, spoon, matches, and tornado powder on your show table.

## Performing the Trick

**1** Start by saying to your audience, **"I have two friends, Sarah and Lawrence, who are archeologists. They spend most of their time exploring ancient ruins and buried cities and tombs. On their expeditions, they sometimes run into great danger, because the people who built these places often left behind booby traps to stop anyone from robbing their ancient treasures. So before every trip they take, I supply Sarah and Lawrence with a magical device of some kind to help protect them. On their last trip, I gave them something I call Freeze-Dried Tornado Powder."**

**2** Hold up the bottle of flour in front of you and say, **"I made this by freezing a tornado, drying it, then crushing it into a powder. If you blow it into the air and heat it up, it will make a tornado. You can control the size of the tornado by the amount of powder you use.**

     **"On their last expedition, Sarah and Lawrence went to an underground tomb in search of three magic jewels called The Three Sisters. I'll show you how they used the Freeze-Dried Tornado Powder to escape a terrible trap after they found the jewels."**

**3** Show the inside of the can to your audience and say, **"This can is like the underground chamber they were in, the three stones are like the jewels, and the candle is like the torch carried by Lawrence to light their way. This tube will let us blow tornado powder into the flame, just the way Sarah did."**

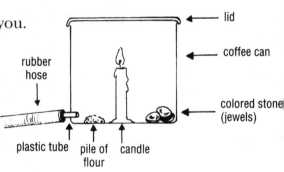

**4** Ask a volunteer to come up and join you.

**5** Place the can on the table. Then, with the spoon, place a small amount of flour inside the can near the tube opening, as shown (B), and say, **"A little tornado will be fine for our demonstration."**

**6** Now light the candle and say, **"When Sarah lifted one of the jewels, it caused a giant stone slab to come down on top of the chamber, trapping them inside. Remembering she had the magical tornado powder I gave her, Sarah quickly threw it into the air, toward the torch Lawrence was carrying. A tornado instantly blew through the chamber, pushing the giant stone slab back into place. Watch!"**

**7** Ask your volunteer to be ready to blow into the rubber tube on your cue. *You and your volunteer should now each put on a pair of goggles.*

**8** Pick up the lid and say, **"Here's the giant stone that came to trap my friends."** Seal the can with the lid, quickly move your hands away, and tell your volunteer to blow (this should be done quickly, before the candle dies out). The top will blow off with a loud BOOM!

*NOTE: Make sure you and your volunteer turn away from the can immediately after the volunteer blows on the rubber tube (C). The lid can blow off with a lot of force, so be careful.*

# SCIENCE

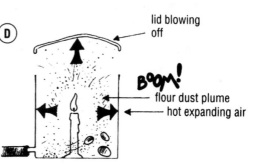

(D)

lid blowing off

BOOM!
— flour dust plume
— hot expanding air

What happened inside your can is a lot like what happens inside a car's engine. Inside an engine, a fuel (gasoline) is first mixed with oxygen ($O_2$) from the air, then heated. The heated gas-air mixture burns extremely fast, creating a tremendous amount of heat that speeds up the surrounding air (see Alien Crush, page 41). This fast-moving air pushes really hard against the car's pistons, which turn the wheels. In your trick, when your volunteer blew on the flour, it mixed with the air in the same way that gas mixes with air in an engine. The candle then heated the flour-air mixture, which burned very rapidly and produced a great deal of heat. The heat sped up the air molecules inside the can, and the speeding molecules then violently blew off the can's lid (D).

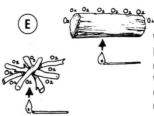

(E)

With a big wooden log, only the outside comes in contact with the heat and oxygen, so it doesn't burn well.

When the log is broken into pieces, heat and oxygen can reach much more of the wood, so it burns very well.

This trick wouldn't work if you tried to burn the pile of flour directly. Nothing would happen—it wouldn't burn. In fact, the trick works *only* if the flour is blown into a fine mist in the air. Why? To understand, think about burning a big wooden log (E). We all know wood burns, but it's almost impossible to light a large log with just a match. Can you guess why? The wood (which is the fuel) first has to be mixed with oxygen and then heated before it will burn. But only the outside of the log comes into contact with the air, and that's not enough. Moreover, it takes more heat than you can get from a single match to adequately heat such a big log.

If you were to break the log into little pieces, not only would the oxygen in the air come in contact with much more of the wood, but the *little* pieces of wood would also be much easier to heat up. And once one piece started to burn, it would provide enough heat to start the next piece nearby burning, and so on. Pretty soon, all the pieces would be burning, creating a tremendous amount of heat. In your trick, blowing the flour into a mist was just like chopping a log into small pieces.

# ✦ mind over matter

**Parental Supervision Required**

*Take a dollar bill that's balanced real still
And don't touch—but try to move it with your mind.
Soon the bill will move about
As if your mind is reaching out
And using forces of an unfamiliar kind.
But it's not really mind over matter—
It's the air nearby that you scatter
That moves the bill in a way to which you're blind.*

## MAGIC

## You Will Need

- large cork
- needle
- new dollar bill
- pliers
- two candles in candle holders
- matches
- table and chairs (with the magical paraphernalia you used in Magic Touch, page 48)
- drinking glass for each member of your audience
- apple or orange juice
- pitcher
- food coloring

## Getting Ready

**1** Using the pliers, and with an adult's help, push the dull end of the needle into the center of the cork so that the sharp end is pointing straight up (be careful not to poke yourself!).

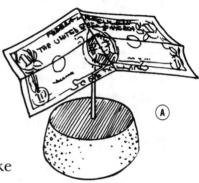

Ⓐ

**2** Fold the dollar bill in half two ways—first left to right, then top to bottom—forming two creases that meet at the exact center of the bill (A).

**3** Pour the juice into the pitcher and mix in the food coloring to make a strange-looking potion.

**4** Set the chairs around the table, then place the unfolded bill, the two candle holders, the matches, the pitcher of colored juice, the glasses, and the cork with the pin in it on the table.

## Performing the Trick

**1** Have your audience members sit at the table, as shown (B). With the help of an adult, light the candles.

**2** Now pour some colored juice into each glass, saying, **"I've been working on a new magic potion that will greatly increase your psychokinetic abilities—** **that is, your ability to move objects with your minds!"**

**3** Have your audience members drink the "magic potion."

**4** Balance the dollar bill on the needle so that the needle point is touching the center of the bill, as shown (B).

**5** Tell one of your audience members to lean close to the dollar bill (about a foot away) and to concentrate really hard on moving it. After a moment, the bill will start to rotate slowly. Repeat this with different members of your audience and see who has the greatest psychokinetic powers!

 SCIENCE

Hey! What's going on here? Why does the dollar bill move if no one is touching it? You set everything up yourself, and you know you didn't hide any string or magnets or other secret stuff to move it. This *must* be a case of mind over matter, right? Not so fast! Remember that before they create some new, really weird idea to explain something unusual, scientists try to explain what they've seen in terms of what they already understand. So let's think the way a scientist thinks. When have you seen something move without being touched? For example, have you ever seen leaves moving across the ground? Is someone's mind controlling the movement of the leaves? Of course not—it's the wind, which is a **current** of air. In any room, there are always tiny currents of air moving about. For instance, the candles heat the air around them, which causes air molecules to speed up, which produces small movements of air.

Your breathing also causes small, circulating patterns of air. Even air coming under the doors from outside or from other rooms causes air currents. While you don't normally notice these small air currents, the delicately balanced dollar bill is extremely sensitive to the slightest push of air. So, even a tiny current of air can cause it to rotate.

# fish-eye lens

**Parental Supervision Required**

*There once was caught a really strange fish,*
*A fish called icthyilofish.*
*It gave me its eye so I'd set it free,*
*And with this eye hidden things I could see.*
*As we said our good-byes and the fish swam away,*
*It winked its one eye as if to say,*
*"I'm fine with one eye—I've made a good deal—*
*For I didn't end up as your evening meal!"*

MAGIC

## You Will Need

- small juice glass with a thick glass base (or a shot glass)
- clear marble, about 1" in diameter
- deck of magic cards, made up of all *one* card, such as the king of spades (these decks are available at magic stores)
- one card from a normal deck, such as the seven of hearts (be sure the card is the same size as the deck of magic cards)
- glass of water
- scissors
- an epoxy-type glue that dries clear
- volunteer

## Getting Ready

**1** Pour about ¼ inch of glue into the bottom of the juice glass, then drop the marble into it as shown and allow the glue to dry (A).

**2** Take one of the cards from the magic deck and cut off the upper left-hand corner. If your deck is all king of spades, this corner piece will have a "K" with a "♠" printed underneath.

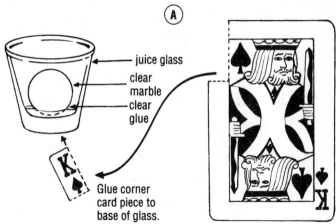

juice glass

clear marble

clear glue

Glue corner card piece to base of glass.

**3** Put a thin layer of the clear glue on the corner card piece (on the side with the "K"), then press it to the bottom of the glass (A). Make sure that no part of this corner piece sticks out beyond the edge of the juice glass. Before gluing, use the scissors to trim off any excess.

**4** Before the glue on the corner piece dries, pour some water into the juice glass until you can see an image of the corner card piece underneath. Then move the card piece around until it is in the center of the glass, right under the marble and in focus. Allow the glue to dry.

**5** Pour out the water and let the inside of the glass dry. Notice that without the water, you cannot see the card piece underneath.

**6** Put the one card from the normal deck on the bottom of the magic deck. When you perform the trick, this will help create the illusion that the magic deck is really just an ordinary deck.

**7** Place the juice glass, the glass of water, and the magic deck (face-down) on your show table.

## Performing the Trick

**1** Pick up the deck of cards with one hand so that the backs of the cards are toward your palm.

**2** Casually show the deck to your audience members, making sure that they see the face of the bottom card (the one different card), while saying, **"I have here a deck of playing cards."**

**3** Then say, **"For this feat of magic, I will need a volunteer,"** and choose a volunteer from the audience to come up and assist you.

**4** Hold the deck so that only the backs of the cards are showing, and spread the cards out like a fan (this is called fanning the deck) (B). Then ask the volunteer to choose just one card and pull it gently out of the deck without letting your audience see what card it is. Then fold the deck back into a pile and put it in your pocket (or somewhere else where no one can see it).

**5** Next, turn your back to the audience and ask the volunteer to show everyone what card he or she has chosen, but without telling (or showing) you. After the audience members have seen the card, tell your volunteer to put it away in a pocket.

**6** Now it's time to tell a story. Say, **"I once caught a great big fish called an icthyilofish. But this was no ordinary fish—the fish spoke to me, telling me that it would give me one of its amazing and strange fish eyes if only I would let it go. The ichthyilofish's eyes could see in all directions at once, even around corners. With such an eye, I could see anything hidden anywhere in the world. So I let the fish swim free, and I now have its magic eye!"**

**7** Have your audience surround the table, and tell them to look down into the juice glass. **"The clear orb you see in the glass is the ichthyilofish's eye. Let's see if I can seek out the face of the card the volunteer chose. Of course, this is a fish's eye, so it works only underwater.** *Look into the eye. . . ."*

**8** Pour the water into the glass, and the image of the corner card piece will appear. Then say, **"Aha! You're hiding the king of spades!"** (Remember to say the card name of the deck you actually have!)

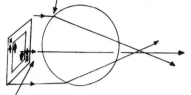

The light waves hitting the marble's surface at an angle are deflected (bent).

The image you see of the card piece is blurred and unrecognizable.

The light waves hitting the marble's surface straight on do not bend.

When light crosses from one kind of material into another, it can bend and change directions (see "Loosing" Your Marbles, page 26). But notice that the light changes direction only when it hits the new material's surface *at an angle*. If the light moves *straight across* the surface, no bending of light occurs.

Look carefully at picture C. The marble's surface is curved, so even though light from the middle of the card piece travels

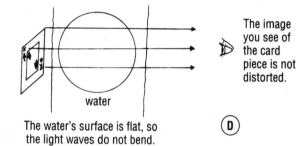

water

The image you see of the card piece is not distorted.

The water's surface is flat, so the light waves do not bend.

straight through the center of the marble, light coming from the card's sides hits the marble's surface at more of an angle. This means that light from the middle of the card travels straight, while light from the card piece's sides is deflected. So, overall, the card piece's image (contained in the light) gets distorted and blurred and you're unable to see it.

Now look at picture D. When you add water to the glass, you create a flat surface for the light to cross. Light from every part of the card can now travel straight across the water's surface, so it doesn't bend. But why doesn't the light bend when it crosses from the water to the glass marble? Remember, in order for light to bend when it crosses from one material into another, it has to enter the second material at an angle *and* has to travel at a different speed. Well, it so happens that light travels through water and glass at very nearly the same speed. So as it crosses from one to the other, even at an angle, it doesn't bend much. Once the light enters the water, it travels straight through the marble and out the other side—so what you see is an undistorted image of the card.

# squeezed space

*When you have poured the waters all*
*Into a space that looks too small,*
*They'll be convinced there's a really weird space,*
*An unseen multidimensional place,*
*Where things come forth or suddenly go,*
*A place of which only wizards know!*
*But the space that looks small isn't so at all—*
*They're betrayed by beliefs they've had since quite small.*

MAGIC

## You Will Need

- two tulip-shaped wineglasses, similar to the ones shown below (to get the most dramatic effect, try experimenting with different shapes of tulip glasses beforehand)

- the mathematical keys you made for 2D or Not 2D, page 30
- pitcher of water
- food coloring (any color)
- stirring spoon

## Getting Ready

**1** Add a few drops of food coloring to the pitcher of water and stir gently.

**2** Now fill one of the glasses all the way to the brim with water.

One glass filled to the brim...

...fills two glasses about three-quarters full.

(A)

68

**3** Carefully pour half of the colored water from the first glass into the second glass until both glasses hold the same amount. It's hard to believe, but both glasses will appear to be about three-quarters full (A).

**4** Put the glasses and the mathematical keys on your show table.

## Performing the Trick

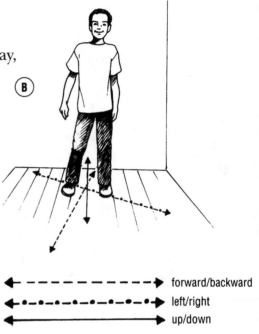

**1** Walk to the table, pick up the keys, and say, **"When magicians make things disappear, where do you suppose those things go? Well, I'm going to now show you one of a wizard's most tightly guarded secrets."** Now lower your voice and move in closer to your audience as you reveal your "secret": **"Our world is called three-dimensional because there are three basic directions—the up/down direction, the forward/back direction, and the left/right direction!"** Demonstrate to your audience what you mean by walking in these directions one by one (B).

forward/backward
left/right
up/down

**2** Now demonstrate the following point by walking through it for your viewers. Say, **"Any place in our 3D space can be reached by moving in a combination of these three directions. For instance, if I move diagonally, I'm traveling in both a forward direction and a right direction. But there exist places in the universe that *cannot* be reached by traveling in any combination of these three directions. These places are called *multidimensional spaces*, and you can reach them only by moving in directions you cannot see."**

**3** Show the key that says 4D Warped Space-Time and say, **"Ahh, but with the right mathematical key, these other dimensions a *wizard* can see! By using this mathematical code, I can squeeze objects into places invisible to you. I can make them . . . disappear!"**

**4** Walk over to the glasses and say, **"Here I have two glasses that are almost full."**

**5** Pick up one glass and say, **"In this first glass, I have much more liquid than could possibly fit into the small space left in this second glass. But by squeezing the excess liquid into another dimension, I can keep the second glass from overflowing—watch!"**

**6** Hold the key near the glass with one hand, and with your other hand pour the water from the first glass into the second. Amazingly, it won't overflow!

# SCIENCE

Have you ever stacked boxes? You can imagine the water in the glass as being made up of a lot of little water boxes. Look at picture C. Suppose you had 40 little water boxes to stack in the glass. The tulip glass is very narrow at the bottom, so you can't fit very many boxes *beside* each other before you have to start stacking boxes *on top of* each other. After stacking 40 boxes, you end up with a very tall, thin stack of water boxes. Now imagine stacking the same 40 boxes in the tip part of the tulip glass. The glass is much wider on top, so you can fit a lot more boxes beside each other before you have to start stacking them on top of each other. So, the same 40 boxes now form a short, wide stack. This is what happened in your trick—a tall, thin column of water in the narrow part of the glass spread out into a short, wide column in the upper part of the glass.

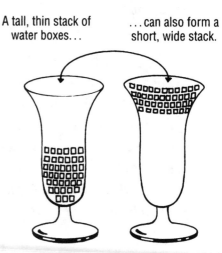

(c)

A tall, thin stack of water boxes...    ...can also form a short, wide stack.

But why does this look so strange? Why does the tall, thin column look as if it contains too much water to fit into the short, wide space? When you're a child, *taller* usually means *bigger*. Tall things are out of reach. Your parents are taller and bigger. Every time you fill an ordinary drinking glass, *more* means *higher*. This feeling is so strong that it makes you think the short space is too small for the tall column of water. A lot of magic tricks work because they fool us by making use of strong feelings and perceptions we have.

# ★ bed of nails

**Parental Supervision Required**

*Like fakirs from India in the time of Aladdin,*
*They lie on sharp nails without any paddin'.*
*On this torturous bed they sleep like a baby—*
*Is it magic that saves them—or just science, maybe?*

MAGIC

## You Will Need

- thick piece of plywood, 1" thick, about 2' wide, and 4' long
- thin piece of plywood, the same width and length but only ½" thick
- several boxes of rustproof nails, 2" long
- two wooden blocks, to be used as a headrest and footrest
- balloon
- tape measure
- pencil or marker
- four wooden blocks, 4" to 5" high
- sheet
- several hammers (making your bed of nails is a group project!)
- adult volunteer, whom you've secretly trained beforehand
- several volunteers

## Getting Ready

*CAUTION! Have only experienced adults hammer nails for you. Or, if you'd like, have an adult show you and your friends how to use a hammer safely, but hammer your bed of nails only with your parents' permission and only under the supervision of an adult.*

*It's also very important that the nails are hammered in straight and are all of the same length (so they stick out the same amount).* **Do not use any old or rusty nails!**

**1** Using the ruler and the pencil or marker, draw a series of lines lengthwise, spaced one inch apart, all the way across the thick piece of plywood.

**2** Draw a second set of lines, also one inch apart, across the width of the board.

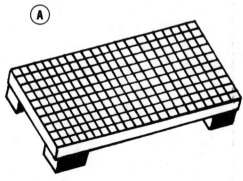

**3** Raise the board off the ground by putting a wooden block under each corner as shown (A). This allows space for the nails to stick through.

**4** Now have a "bed of nails" party. At each point where two lines intersect, hammer a nail until its head is flat against the plywood surface (B). Get some friends and adults to help. When you're finished, store the bed of nails facedown so that no one can fall or step on the nails.

**5** Practice this trick with the adult whom you have chosen to be your "volunteer." Just before performing the trick, cover the bed of nails with the sheet.

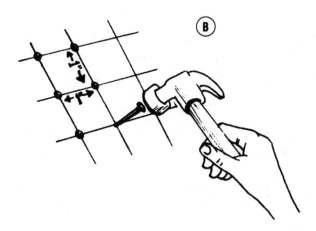

## Performing the Trick

**1** Look at your audience and say, **"I was on what seemed like the longest walk of my life through a vast and barren desert in India. I was so tired I couldn't see straight. I finally came upon an ancient Indian palace. I thought to myself, now I can finally get some sleep and maybe some ice cream, too! When I went inside I was greeted by an old Indian fakir—that's the Indian word for wizard. The fakir told me I was welcome to spend the night, and he led me to a room where he said I could sleep."**

**2** Draw your audience's attention to the sheet-covered bed on the floor and say, **"Here's the bed the Indian fakir gave me to sleep on. Looks comfortable, don't you think?"**

**3** Now quickly pull off the sheet to reveal the sharp nails underneath, while saying. **"Well, that sneaky fakir had given me a bed of the sharpest nails I'd ever seen! I think he sensed I was a fellow wizard and wanted to test my powers. Much to his surprise, I slept quite well on that torturous bed! In the morning, while we ate a breakfast of the most fabulous ice cream (for the fakir was also a great lover of ice cream), we laughed about his sneaky trick."**

**4** Now say, **"For me, sleeping on a bed of nails is a simple thing—I am a magician, after all. But now I'm going to show all of you how to do it in case you should meet up with a sneaky Indian wizard, too."**

**5** Ask for three volunteers to come up. Remember that one of these volunteers needs to be the adult with whom you've secretly practiced this trick beforehand. This is the volunteer who will lie on the bed of nails.

**6** To show how sharp the nails are, blow up the balloon until it is full, then push it into one of the corner nails to pop it. Say, **"Boy, these nails are really sharp!"**

**7** Now stand in front of the adult volunteer and say, **"It's important to first put yourself in a hypnotic trance. In this trance, I want you to make your skin take on the properties of steel. As long as you remain in this trance, no nail will be able to penetrate you. Watch closely."**

**8** Look at the adult assistant intensely and say, **"Let go of all fear, for your skin is becoming as strong as steel. Let go!"** Your assistant should pretend to look sleepy (practice this with your assistant beforehand).

**9** Ask the two other volunteers to each grab one of the adult's arms. Then have your "sleepy" assistant gently sit on one end of the nail bed and slowly lie back (C). The other volunteers should keep the sleeper from falling back on the nails too quickly.

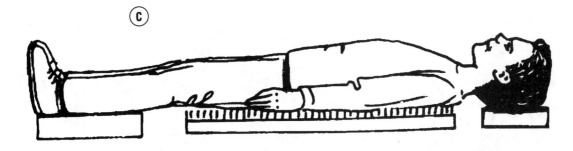

**10** After your "sleeping" assistant has been lying on the bed for a moment or so, carefully place the thin piece of plywood on top, as shown, and have someone small carefully step on top (D). Say, **"Now you *all* know how to get a good night's sleep on a bed of nails!"**

## SCIENCE

Ohhh! That looks as though it would hurt! Why doesn't it? The secret to the bed of nails is very simple. Take a nail exactly like the ones in your bed and very lightly press the sharp end against the palm of your hand. Now push on the nail a little harder, but not enough to hurt yourself. What have you learned? If a nail doesn't press against you very hard, it won't hurt or puncture you. The secret of the bed of nails is that the weight of your body is shared by so many nails. So, each of the hundreds of nails supports only a very tiny fraction of a person's total body weight. The small amount of pressure on each individual nail isn't enough for that nail to harm someone lying on a bed of nails. The more nails, the better!

# Glossary of Science Terms

**air pressure:** The downward force put forth by the weight of the earth's atmosphere.

**atom:** The smallest particle or unit of matter that exists and cannot be divided. Atoms are made up of protons, neutrons, and electrons.

**charge:** The quantity of electricity that an object possesses. A surplus or shortage of electrons in an object determines whether it has a positive or negative charge.

**current:** A fluid body, such as air or water, that flows continuously in a specific direction.

**electron:** A particle of matter that is negatively charged. Electrons are found in atoms.

**fluid:** A substance such as a liquid or gas whose molecules flow freely. It has no fixed shape and tends to conform to the outline of its container.

**gravity:** The force that attracts or pulls objects in space to one another.

**inertia:** The property of a substance that causes it to remain at rest or continue to move in the same straight line unless acted upon by an external force.

**interval:** A period of time between one event or occurrence and the next.

**molecule:** The smallest particle of a substance that can exist independently. A molecule is composed of one or more atoms.

**neutron:** A particle of matter that is neither positively nor negatively charged. Neutrons are found in atoms.

**particle:** An extremely small portion or amount of something.

**property:** A characteristic quality or distinctive trait belonging to an individual or thing.

**proton:** A particle of matter that is positively charged. Protons are found in atoms.

**steam:** The vapor into which water converts when it is boiled.

# Glossary of Magic Terms

*In order to help familiarize you with some magic terms, we have included this short glossary. Some of the definitions listed here relate to activities in this book, while others are included to improve and expand your magic vocabulary.*

**effect:** The action the audience witnesses during a magic trick; what the audience sees, or the magic trick itself.

**force:** A technique used, usually in card magic, to cause a volunteer to make a specific selection. The performer knows the identity of the selection beforehand.

**illusion:** Something that is not as it appears.

**mentalism:** The branch of magic dealing with tricks involving the mind. Mind reading, ESP, clairvoyance, telekinesis, and telepathy fall into this category.

**misdirection:** The art of redirecting your audience's attention; making them look where you want them to look using either verbal or physical means.

**palming:** The technique of secretly hiding something in your hand while at the same time keeping your hand in a natural-looking position. If performed properly, the hidden object is never detected.

**sleight of hand:** Another name for close-up magic, especially close-up magic with cards and coins.

**vanish:** A trick in which someone or something apparently disappears into thin air.

# ✦ Index